tenor saxophone

Now you can be the feature tenor saxophone soloist on eight specially recorded arrangements

Christmas SONGS

TAKE THE LEAD

tenor saxophone

IMP

International MUSIC Publications

International Music Publications Limited
Griffin House 161 Hammersmith Road London W6 8BS England

GW00671702

Series Editors: Sadie Cook and Anna Joyce

Editorial, production and recording: Artemis Music Limited
Design and production: Space DPS Limited

Published 2000

International MUSIC Publications

© International Music Publications Limited
Griffin House 161 Hammersmith Road London W6 8BS England

IMP

International Music Publications Limited

England: Griffin House
                  161 Hammersmith Road
                  London W6 8BS

Germany: Marstallstr. 8
                  D-80539 München

Denmark: Danmusik
                  Vognmagergade 7
                  DK1120 Copenhagen K

Carisch

Italy: Nuova Carisch Srl
                  Via Campania 12
                  20098 San Giuliano Milanese
                  Milano

Spain: Nueva Carisch España
                  Magallanes 25
                  28015 Madrid

France: Carisch Musicom
                  25 Rue d'Hauteville
                  75010 Paris

tenor saxophone

TAKE THE LEAD

In the Book...

On the CD...

The Christmas Song
(Chestnuts Roasting On An Open Fire)

Words and Music by
Mel Torme and Robert Wells

Demonstration

Backing

Moderately

Demonstration   Backing

Frosty The Snowman

Words and Music by
Jack Rollins and Steve Nelson

Have Yourself A Merry Little Christmas

Demonstration

Backing

Words and Music by
Ralph Blane and Hugh Martin

slower

Little Donkey

Demonstration

Backing

Words and Music by Eric Boswell

Rudolph The
Red-Nosed Reindeer

Words and Music by Johnny Marks

Santa Claus
Is Comin' To Town

Demonstration   Backing

Words by Haven Gillespie
Music by J Fred Coots

18

Sleigh Ride

Words by Mitchell Parish
Music by Leroy Anderson

21

Demonstration   Backing

Winter Wonderland

Words by Dick Smith
Music by Felix Bernard

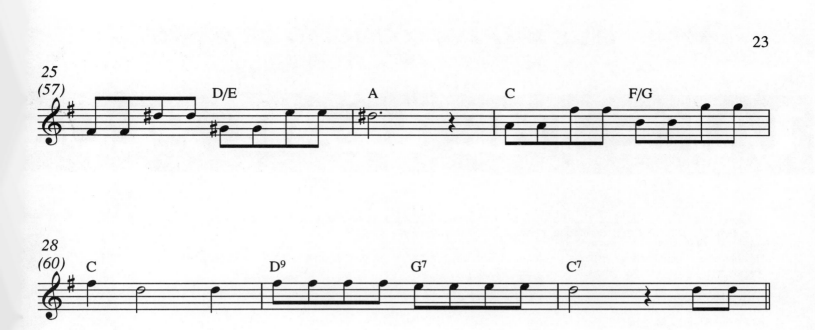

Printed and bound in Great Britain

Whatever your instrument is...
you can now

TAKE THE LEAD *PLUS*

- Available in C, Bb, Eb and Bass Clef editions, this new concept opens up Take The Lead to a wider range of instruments, including cello, trombone, bassoon and baritone saxophone

- Flexible arrangements allowing players to team up with any number of instruments able to read from one of the 4 editions – C, Bb, Eb and Bass Clef.

- Each edition contains the full instrumental score in either 2,3 or 4 parts

- Professionally recorded backing tracks that re-create the sound of the original recordings.

TAKE THE LEAD

- Each book comes with a professionally recorded CD containing full backing tracks for you to play along with, and demonstration tracks to help you learn the songs

- Ideal for solo or ensemble use - in each edition, songs are in the same concert pitch key

- Each book includes carefully selected and edited top line arrangements; chord symbols in concert pitch for use by piano or guitar

- Suitable for intermediate players
  "A great way to get some relaxing playing done in between the serious stuff" **Sheet Music Magazine**

Discover The Lead

- This new 'spin off' of the Take The Lead series is ideal for beginners of all ages, grades 1-3

- The books contain simplified arrangements of well-known tunes to help the beginner develop reading and playing skills, while increasing confidence as a soloist

- Includes a useful fingering chart plus a CD with full backing and demonstration tracks

- Lots of helpful hints and technical tips to help you get to know your instrument

SHARE THE LEAD

- All pieces have been carefully selected and arranged at an easy level to provide fun material for today's instrumentalists

- All the arrangements work not only as duets for one particular instrument, but with all other instruments in the series (i.e. the flute book works with the clarinet book)

- The professionally recorded CD allows you to hear each song in 4 different ways – a complete demonstration of the track; part two plus backing so you can play along on part one; part one plus backing so you can play along on part two; and the backing only so you and a friend can Share The Lead!